# Praise for This Book

This wonderful handbook on alcoholism is the best, most concise text I have ever come across in the more than forty-five years I have worked in the field in the United States and Southeast Asia. It is accurate, hopeful, and instructive for both the person with addictions and their family members. I was particularly impressed with the information on interventions, which is useful for both families and professionals.

*Marjorie Nixon, LCSW,*
*Addiction Specialist*
*and in Recovery a Day at a Time*

This book will bring help to people having trouble with their alcohol use by explaining the concept of alcohol addiction and showing a way to recover from this devastating disease so they can regain life to its fullest. More important, it provides a roadmap for family members, loved ones, and friends of the person addicted to alcohol to help him or her. It gives great hope and explains how family members can live life without the devastation that a loved one can bring to a family when alcohol takes over.

*Br. Gerry Patin, CSsR*

# Alcohol Abuse

## RECOVERY FOR THE CATHOLIC FAMILY

FATHER TED LAWSON, CSsR

Liguori
PUBLICATIONS
A Redemptorist Ministry

*Imprimi Potest:* Kevin Zubel, CSsR, Provincial
Denver Province, the Redemptorists

Published by Liguori Publications, Liguori, Missouri 63057
Liguori Publications, a nonprofit corporation, is an apostolate of the Redemptorists (Redemptorists.com).

*Phone:* 800-325-9521 *Web:* Liguori.org

*Alcohol Abuse: Recovery for the Catholic Family*


ISBN 978-0-7648-2864-5
E-ISBN: 978-0-7648-7247-1

Library of Congress Control Number: 2023949237



Printed in the United States of America
27 26 25 24 23 / 5 4 3 2 1
First Edition

Cover design: Wendy Barnes
Cover illustration: Love You Stock/Shutterstock

# Contents

# The Intervention

## Real Friends Help Shut Out a Toxic "Friend"

One morning at 7:30, I received a note from a boss that I was to attend a meeting with him and his bosses. That afternoon, I walked into a room of friends and acquaintances but had no idea what was about to take place.

This is my own real example of an *intervention*. For several hours, I listened to friends and fellow employees explain how my drinking had affected their lives and our work environment. I heard alternatives about how this situation would play out. I was told, "You will enter a thirty-day treatment program for alcoholism, and after you complete this program and establish a program of non-consumption of any alcohol, you will return to work with your employment intact."

After I agreed to their terms, I walked back to my office, and called my sister to tell her what had happened. She is in the Alcoholics Anonymous program, so I sought her advice. She asked if I believed I was an alcoholic, and I said, "After listening to all that was said at the intervention, yes." She said, "If you don't believe it, walk away and find another job." My sister was saying that if I wasn't committed, I would most likely fail.

I completed my thirty days of treatment, took some vacation at home, and then I returned to work.

After I stopped drinking, I began to regularly attend AA meetings and live a sober life one day at a time. I began to change as I adopted a life steeped in AA sobriety and filled with AA friends and values.

I attended 6 AM meetings each day of the week on the way to work. New horizons of friendship and familiarity with a variety of people were among the gifts. After a while, I was selected by the membership to chair the Wednesday meeting. The usual time to be chair was about six months, but I ran the meeting for five years. Through those years, I grew to know many members. There was constant growth and change as members came and went.

Leaving behind one of my closest friends, alcohol, was difficult, but discovering a life of freedom and newness was wonderful and productive.

I didn't fully realize it at the time, but that intervention gave me a chance to correct my life. My employer valued my talent and stood by me.

I have been sober for more than forty years. Thank God the people in my life—my *real* friends—saw something in me that I didn't even see in myself.

*Fr. Denis Ryan, CSsR*

# Preface

Anger, fear, and despair reign when alcohol abuse is in charge. Chaos is the constant state of life of alcohol abusers and their loved ones. Life may feel hopeless. It is not. There is help. If you are mired in the morass of alcohol abuse, either as the drinker or as his or her loved one, this book is for you.

Different words are used to discuss and define alcohol abuse and the people who abuse it. While "alcohol use disorder (AUD)" is the name that professionals today attach to the disease, I will use the more common terms—alcoholism and alcoholic.

I write from a solid Catholic perspective. I am a longtime Catholic priest with extensive education in addiction counseling. My aim is to define the crippling disease of alcoholism, describe its impact on the family, and offer ideas for how to get help. My book is not a definitive presentation on alcoholism. I pray that it's useful.

People struggling with alcoholism (or other addictive behaviors) may be the last to realize they have a problem. Alcoholism can destroy the lives of everyone living with or dealing with an alcoholic, who can be of any age, race, gender, societal class, religion.

Those addicted to alcohol and those who live with them wonder, “What’s going on? I’m afraid. I’m angry. What can I do? I’m not living, I’m surviving.” If that’s you or someone you care about, your next job is to find HELP. This beautiful prayer by Reinhold Niebuhr outlines a helpful path.

God grant me the serenity
to accept the things I cannot change,
courage to change the things I can,
and wisdom to know the difference.

**Serenity** means finding peace of mind and a healthy perspective. That comes about when we **accept** or understand that we are powerless in certain areas of our lives. Finding **courage** to change comes with realizing we are not always powerless and we can act to make a difference. **Wisdom** is growing in our ability to make healthy choices and ask for help.

The Serenity Prayer is true. It comforts. Pray it daily. It’s an important ingredient in the recipe for the recovery God wants for you.

Alcoholics will find their best starting point is the Twelve Steps of Alcoholics Anonymous, a program I discuss in these pages. AA opens the door to a fulfilling life without alcohol. Similar help is available to the loved ones of the alcoholic. With the help of God and resources like this book, recovery can be yours. Let’s begin.

Chapter One

# The Erosion of Lives and Relationships

# The Erosion of Lives and Relationships

*As for me and my household, we will serve the* L*ORD.*

JOSHUA 24:15B

What would it be like to have an active volcano one hundred yards from your home? You would never know when the volcano will erupt and destroy everything you own and everyone you love. You live with this constant threat that life as you know it could drastically change at any time. You might respond by developing various plans to minimize the inevitable impending disaster. Eventually, however, you would see that plans are useless due to the strength of the volcano. You might try to ignore it and live as if it didn't exist. This approach wouldn't work because, deep down, you'd know this omnipresent specter of destruction remains. How long could you live with the uncertainty?

The tension of this scenario is like that experienced by an alcoholic and members of his or her family. It describes the silent, unwanted third party that has infiltrated the family, controlling everyone it encounters. The name of this third party? Alcoholism. Left unchecked, this disease kills. This killer can be stopped, but first it must be known.

## Alcoholism Defined

Defining the disease of alcoholism is difficult. The key word to remember is *disease*. Unchecked, the disease of alcoholism is chronic, progressive, and fatal. Here's a definition:

> *Alcoholism is a chemical dependence, a chronic disease characterized by an individual's inability to control his or her intake of mood-altering chemicals. That uncontrolled intake causes dysfunction in all facets of the alcoholic's life.*

Let's consider each part of this definition separately.

*Alcoholism is a chemical dependence, a chronic disease.* It can be compared to diabetes. The diabetic's body cannot deal with sugar properly. It never will be able to deal with sugar properly. A diabetic will always be a diabetic. With a proper diet and, in some cases medication, the person can live a healthy life. Likewise, the alcoholic's body cannot process alcohol in the same way as someone who does not have the disease. Despite all resolutions and attempts to set limits on his or her drinking, without intervention, the alcoholic constantly breaks these limits.

The drinker is unable to *control his or her intake of mood-altering chemicals, causing dysfunction in all facets of the alcoholic's life.*

For example, after a few drinks, Jim is the life of the party. Lately, he finds he consistently has more drinks than he intended to have. Before the office Christmas party, he had decided to have only two drinks. But a couple of hours into the party, Jim is not sure how much he has had to drink. While he is the life of the party, he has far exceeded the limit he set for himself. After several incidents like this, Jim realizes deep down that he cannot control how much he drinks—or even when he drinks.

Note that the definition of alcoholism uses the phrase "mood-altering chemicals," not alcohol. Alcohol (technically, ethanol or ethyl alcohol) is a drug that the body can become dependent upon. There are, of course, many drugs that a person can become addicted to, but alcoholism is one of the most common addictions and continues to grow.

Joan, through her use of another drug, realized she was an alcoholic. Under pressure about her drinking at home and at work, she admitted she had a problem and decided to quit drinking. While abstaining from alcohol, Joan found that stress still mounted in her life. Her doctor prescribed Valium (diazepam), a drug whose effect on the body is similar to that of alcohol. On her own, she soon began to increase the dosage her doctor had specified. For a period of time, Joan failed to realize or admit that she was looking for something to take the place of the alcohol she had given up.

While addiction to drugs such as Oxycodone, heroin,

and PCP is a major, growing problem in our society, this book will focus on alcohol. The number of alcoholics in this country shows that for too many it is a drug of choice.

One form of alcohol is no more or no less addictive than another. Many think alcoholics only drink hard liquor (whiskey, gin, vodka, etc.), but beer and wine drinkers are still drinking alcohol and can still get addicted.

It helps to know that alcoholism is a biopsychosocial disease. "Bio" refers to the body's physical response to the chemical. "Psychosocial" refers to the effects of the disease that are not purely physical. Four different areas of the alcoholic's life are affected: physical, psychological, social, and spiritual. These are what are referenced as "facets of the alcoholic's life" in the definition.

## Alcoholism: A Snapshot

In a 2019 study by the National Institute on Alcohol Abuse and Alcoholics, 25.8 percent of persons ages eighteen and older reported engaging in binge drinking and/or "heavy alcohol use" in the past month. If these people are alcoholics, each one has a direct impact on the lives of at least four other people. Mathematically, 25.8 percent of a group of 1,000 people brings the total number of alcoholics to 258. Thus, they are affecting about 1,000 persons with this destructive disease.

Alcoholism does not discriminate. The alcoholic can be a mother, father, daughter, son, sister, brother, aunt, uncle, grandparent, or friend. Not every family fits into the mold of a traditional nuclear model. More homes today are headed by single parents, comprised of blended families, or multiple generations. While this book will discuss the traditional family structure, my primary focus is on the erosion of lives and relationships due to alcoholism. No matter how a family is constructed, no household with an alcoholic is exempt, and the effects are, devastatingly, the same.

## Facets of a Disease

An alcoholic's body cannot handle alcohol. The chemical alters his or her physical makeup. The alcoholic's body absorbs alcohol more easily than it absorbs essential nutrients. The human body can only take so much. After a time, it breaks down. This physical difference in the ability to absorb alcohol is difficult to observe. For all practical purposes, the alcoholic may appear to drink in the same way other people do. In fact, in the early stages of the disease, the alcoholic will be able to drink more than others. This is called "increased tolerance."

He or she can drink everyone else "under the table" and appear completely sober. Alcohol is a powerful drug that can kill if someone takes too much at one time. Withdrawal from alcohol also can be life-threatening. The "shakes" that alcoholics suffer when they quit drinking is a withdrawal symptom.

Medically, alcohol is classified as a depressant. It slows or numbs the body's central nervous system. The first response of many people in a crisis is to have a drink to settle their nerves. In movies, it's common to see a character go for the bottle when times are tough. In life, after a certain number of drinks, the resulting numbness or a related state becomes the status quo. As the brain's operations are dulled, impaired thinking sets in, adversely affecting the psychological facet of life.

For example, consider Karen. She has a stress-filled job as a sales rep for a large corporation. Financial worries about her upcoming wedding hang over her head. Her fiancé often tells her she should find a way to relax. Karen is convinced that the best way to relieve her tension is to have a few drinks. That decision may plague her. Later in life, Karen may find alcohol is the only way she has to deal with life's struggles.

When an alcoholic is actively drinking, the people he or she interacts with notice the change. They may show concern, nag, or express anger and resentment. The alcoholic will begin to associate with people who don't care about his or her drinking or may even affirm it. Sometimes these may be people the alcoholic would not otherwise interact with. Companions who value drinking and have no regard for its consequences reinforce the alcoholic's behavior. In this way the social facet of the alcoholic's life is altered by the disease.

For example, Jack likes to drink with the guys from the office. Every day after work they stop at a bar across the street to have "one for the road" before heading home. Jack, however, has a few more than one, and his friends challenge his behavior. Rather than put up with their objections, Jack steams and finds a different place to go after work where he can drink as much as he wants without judgment. There, Jack becomes loud, and the management looks unkindly toward him. Eventually, he finds the best place to drink is at home in the privacy of his basement workroom. Little by little, Jack cuts himself off from other people so he doesn't have to worry about others questioning his drinking.

Isolation, which accompanies many drinkers, affects the spiritual facet of an alcoholic's life. Spirituality is not necessarily connected with formal religion. The spiritual aspect of life is wherever people—including alcoholics—look for strength, help, or solutions to the realities of life.

For instance, Patti is in her early forties. For as long as

she can remember, she has received praise for her leadership skills. When she was in school, she was active in student government. At home, her five younger brothers and sisters always looked to her for help and guidance. When she began her career, it didn't take long for her employer to see that she was hard-working and responsible. Through the years she was rewarded with several significant promotions.

As her brothers and sisters reached adulthood and moved out on their own, they continued to turn to Patti for help. Patti believes she should be in charge and have the answers. At the same time, she has found she is unable to solve every problem or always offer direction.

Patti finds she cannot erase her sister's pain when she experiences the tragic death of her husband. Patti cannot dissuade her employer from selling the company to a larger corporation. Patti cannot make the man she is in love with love her back. She feels powerful when she is in charge, and alcohol seduces her, relaxing her so she can delude herself into believing she is in charge. Her go-to way of dealing with realities outside her control becomes more frequent drinking. When her power mindset does not fit a particular life situation, the only thing she can turn to is alcohol.

## Cause and Effect

The spiritual facet of alcoholism, the most difficult to recognize and define, is responsible for an individual's will to live. We accept or deny values, goals, and limitations in the context of our spiritual facet. Life can be a mere survival of daily events, or it can be an exciting gift to be relished, depending upon the extent to which we are in touch with our spiritual facet.

For alcoholics, the need to drink is more important than being with other people. In the case of some alcoholics, that need also will determine what kind of people the alcoholic will associate with. Alcohol can give the alcoholic the illusion of power or control. The alcoholic knows that if she or he drinks enough, a desired state of consciousness will be achieved. The illusion of life-sustaining strength is found in the bottle. It is difficult, if not impossible, to deal effectively with the spiritual facet of life under these circumstances.

The spiritual facet of life includes handling as best we can the daily realities that are outside of our control. As the alcoholic struggles to cope with human limitations, daily problems, and questions with no cut-and-dried answers, a drink becomes the starting point for an attempted resolution. Use of the chemical provides the primary means of dealing with life. It's a crutch.

The alcoholic's goals and values deteriorate as the need for alcohol increases. Permanent brain damage due to alcohol or death are prospects for the alcoholic who is not in recovery and never gets treatment. Early death, rather than brain injury, is more likely in store for the untreated alcoholic. Death may come from the constant and extended presence of alcohol in the body, as the body eventually breaks down when a foreign substance such as alcohol continually bombards it. More often, though, death is caused by accidents or conflicts that result from drinking.

Think for a moment of the number of traffic deaths reported where the use of alcohol is mentioned or suspected. There are charts and graphs explaining the progression of alcoholism in scientific terms. When all is said and done, however, these charts show a beginning and an end to the disease. Looking at the ways in which alcoholism affects the four facets of life is one way of explaining that progression.

## A Progressive Disease

The image of a footbridge illustrates the disease's progression. Imagine that the walkway of the bridge represents the physical facet of the person. The lower support on the right represents the psychological facet, and the support on the left side represents the social facet. The railing symbolizes the spiritual facet. This bridge is weak because it is not being maintained, and it eventually breaks down. While the whole bridge deteriorates at the same time, different parts will weaken faster than others. The first part of the bridge to show signs of wearing down is the railing, which guides and steadies those who use it. It will get shaky and eventually fall off.

The first facet of the alcoholic's life to fall apart is the spiritual. In the beginning, the alcohol gives the illusion that everything is under control. The desired response or mood is achieved when a particular amount of the chemical is consumed. However, those feelings only last as long as the alcohol is working in the body.

The chemical brings about a false sense of power and security. Limitations and feelings of inadequacy return once alcohol leaves the scene. The next area of the bridge to break down is the support system. The use of alcohol becomes the major ingredient in the alcoholic's interaction with others. When the people who are close to the alcoholic can no longer handle the drinking, the alcoholic has to find people who are tolerant or drink alone.

When one support of the bridge breaks down, the others will follow. The psychological facet breaks down when the alcoholic realizes that the drinking has isolated him or her. The drinking brings about behavior and events that fill the alcoholic with guilt, shame, and fear. Guilt sets in over mistakes and irresponsible behavior. Shame develops through a belief that he or she is no good. Fear that others may discover these secrets further isolates the alcoholic. The last part of the bridge to break down is the walkway. Without supports, it is only a matter of time before the bridge can no longer hold anything. The alcoholic's body cannot be abused by the chemical indefinitely. Major organs and body functions are impaired or even stop after a time. The results are compromised health or death.

If a person's drinking is causing a problem, that person needs help. There may be periods when she or he can abstain from alcohol, but when problems resurface and the drinking returns, help is still needed.

Now that we have defined the disease and summarized some of its effects, it's important to examine the problems caused by excess drinking. The alcoholic and the people the alcoholic encounters must cope with many of the same issues. That's chapter two's focus.

Chapter Two

# Understanding the Alcoholic

# Understanding the Alcoholic

*[Jesus said,]*
*"Those who are well do not need a physician, but the sick do. I did not come to call the righteous but sinners."*

MARK 2:17

The disease of alcoholism often is not recognized as an illness because of misconceptions that cloud people's minds. For some, *alcoholic* carries the same connotations—or worse—that *leper* did in biblical times. Those who think this way—often including the alcoholic himself or herself—consider alcoholics to be weak or inferior. They may view the alcoholic's misfortunes as a punishment from God.

## Myths Unraveled

Three common myths some people believe about this disease are:

***Myth 1: Only certain people can be alcoholics.***

Alcoholism is an equal-opportunity disease. It has no regard for race, age, religion, sex, or socioeconomic status. Some observers may identify unkempt people without homes who aimlessly walk the streets as alcoholics, but that presumption would not necessarily be right.

Many active alcoholics hold jobs and rarely miss a day of work, although the job may be new because of problems from previous employment. By all outward appearances, these alcoholics may seem to have ideal families, social positions, and financial security. But the real picture is far from ideal. The multiple conflicts in their lives are not always readily apparent to the casual observer.

Much of the literature on alcoholism uses the pronoun "he" in referring to the alcoholic. This seriously limits people's understanding of who can be an alcoholic. Millions of women suffer from alcoholism. Until recently, it was assumed that alcoholism developed and progressed identically in both men and women. Researchers now know that, because of their different biological makeup, women process alcohol more rapidly than men. As a result, women typically become addicted more quickly, and the life-threatening aspects of alcoholism tend to progress faster in them. In addition, heavy alcohol use by pregnant women can result in a serious condition in their children known as fetal alcohol syndrome.

Despite increased awareness of sexist language and behavior, a double standard still exists in our culture around acceptable behavior for men and women. Some still think a man who drinks to excess is a "man's man." But they don't think so positively about women, who get placed under a much harsher microscope.

This dual standard can have tragic results for women, who are forced to deal with serious life issues such as rape, incest, physical abuse, and emotional abuse. Combine those issues with an environment or family background where alcohol is "the great sedative" and the stage is set for disease development and many other disastrous problems.

Plus, alcoholism often afflicts people under the legal drinking age. The disease progresses faster in young, still-developing brains and bodies. While youthful drinking or the use of other mood-altering chemicals can be seen as experimental or "sowing wild oats," it is problematic if an adolescent becomes chemically dependent. Drinking and drug use among teens can't be ignored. This book focuses on adult alcoholism, but underage drinking is also a serious problem, and addiction in children and teens should be addressed in our society.

***Myth 2: The alcoholic is spineless or weak.***

This is one of the toughest myths to debunk, for it fits hand in hand with the false, outdated idea that alcoholism is not a disease. Our culture still presents the ideal of the "rugged individual" as a criterion by which to judge others and ourselves. This falsity reinforces the need for control or "having it all together." People with this mindset believe we should be able to handle any problem if we are tough enough. Many feel severe guilt when they can't meet this tough standard.

When the chemical is in charge of an alcoholic, promises to others are broken, trust is lost, and lives are disrupted. It is only natural for others to be hurt by the consequences of the disease, especially if it is seen as a weakness and not an illness. A powerful way to succinctly explain alcoholism as a disease is to add the suffix "ism" (used in defining behavior) to the key word:

**ALCOHOL + ISM = ALCOHOLISM**

By itself, alcohol has little power. But when it interacts with the four facets of human existence, it takes on a great deal of power. The three letters at the end of the word *alcoholism*—"ism"—constitute the most noticeable part of the disease. Complete the equation, remove the chemical, and the alcoholic's physical, psychological, social, and spiritual facets will *still* be affected by the disease detrimentally.

Steve quit drinking about three months ago. However, the only real change in his life is that there is no longer any alcohol in his body. He feels most at ease when he is alone. He finds it difficult to deal with the stress at his job. He lashes out increasingly at his family. He is frustrated because his thinking is muddled or clouded most of the time. At times he even questions the point of continuing such a hopeless life.

Steve may have quit drinking, but his life is still controlled by alcohol. He hasn't found a way to live without alcohol as a constant companion. In common parlance, Steve is a "dry drunk." Yet he knows he cannot handle alcohol in the same way others can. Until he seeks and finds help outside himself, his struggle will go on.

***Myth 3: Once this stressful period ends or certain problems are solved, the drinking will stop.***

The reality, of course, is that when one reason or excuse for drinking disappears, another *will* take its place. This third myth is merely a form of denial, the primary roadblock to recognizing alcoholism. To continue drinking, alcoholics protect themselves from the truth by resorting to denials of all kinds: rationalizations, lying, even feigned ignorance. In the mind of the active, denying alcoholic, truth that is denied need not be faced.

Chuck realized he was an alcoholic when he allowed himself to see that his life was falling apart. Excuses he used in the past were no longer holding up. His boss was always badgering him about the number of martinis he had during lunch and at meetings, so he changed jobs. The new job was much better until the same pattern started happening. He decided he was not cut out to be an employee, so he quit the second job and started his own business out of his home.

Upon spending more time at home, Chuck realized

his wife was always hounding him about something, usually his drinking. Her nagging got so bad that he finally told her he wanted a divorce. She agreed and moved out. When Chuck was able to drink without anyone to criticize him, he realized how much he was drinking and that his drinking was out of control. Drinking had become his major priority, and he had been willing to sacrifice his family and career for it.

As his disease progressed, Chuck had been able to find excuses for his drinking. He was able to see that he needed help only when he could no longer find any reasons but alcoholism to explain the point he had reached.

Chuck's story offers a framework for the role denial plays in the progression of the disease. If excuses, rationalizations, or avoidance of the issues get in the way, the alcoholic's future looks grim.

One of the first things alcoholics must learn is they cannot recover from the disease by themselves. Alcoholics Anonymous (AA), founded in 1935, is a group of people who come together to help one another take a stand against this disease. All of them have walked a similar road. They are all alcoholics.

## The AA Twelve-Step Program

Rigorous honesty is a hallmark premise of AA. In an honest environment, myths like the ones outlined in this book lose their power to deceive. AA members are willing to go to almost any length to maintain sobriety. For them, sobriety is more than complete abstinence from alcohol. It is a change in lifestyle. An alcoholic seeking sobriety in AA will need to ask others for help and be prepared to accept it.

Alcoholics Anonymous is based on working these Twelve Steps.

1. We admitted we were powerless over alcohol —that our lives had become unmanageable.
2. Came to believe that a Power greater than ourselves could restore us to sanity.
3. Made a decision to turn our will and our lives over to the care of God as we understood Him.
4. Made a searching and fearless moral inventory of ourselves.
5. Admitted to God, to ourselves, and to another human being the exact nature of our wrongs.

6. Were entirely ready to have God remove all these defects of character.
7. Humbly asked Him to remove our shortcomings.
8. Made a list of all persons we had harmed, and became willing to make amends to them all.
9. Made direct amends to such people wherever possible, except when to do so would injure them or others.
10. Continued to take personal inventory and when we were wrong promptly admitted it.
11. Sought through prayer and meditation to improve our conscious contact with God as we understood Him, praying only for knowledge of His will for us and the power to carry that out.
12. Having had a spiritual awakening as the result of these Steps, we tried to carry this message to alcoholics, and to practice these principles in all our affairs.

*Source:* Verbatim from *AA.org*

## Faith in Action

The AA program calls upon the alcoholic to meet the disease head on. Importantly, this confrontation is not done alone. All steps are approached within the framework of the group. The alcoholic meets, listens, and talks with others who have lived through the same hell.

AA has helped millions get sober and stay sober. AA and those associated with it, such as those who attend meetings, can help the alcoholic achieve what he or she cannot achieve alone. Sobriety. The program stresses powerlessness over alcohol, honesty, surrender to a higher power, and asking for help.

The first step is an honest recognition that life is out of control. Those who conclude that this first step is true for them know that life has gotten worse, and efforts to make it better have failed. The alcoholic must look for help outside himself or herself.

Those working this program are called to rely heavily on their higher power. Some choose to call the power "God." There is no formal definition for "higher power." AA stands firm on its tradition not to be affiliated with any formal religion. Rather, AA helps the alcoholic by creating a safe and honest environment.

That first AA meeting can be frightening. Since anonymity is a main tenet of the group, it is difficult even to guess what kind of people will be at the meeting. A person calling the telephone number for "Alcoholics Anonymous" will find a supportive person at the other end of the line who will offer to send someone to meet and walk into the meeting with the newcomer.

This first step may appear impossible to take. While it may be difficult to ask for help, it is even more difficult to accept it. AA does not offer a *cure*—an alcoholic will remain an alcoholic for life. AA offers *recovery*—a way to live well with the disease. Newcomers are urged to keep coming back to meetings. The disease did not develop overnight, and the same is true of recovery. Recovery takes time and effort, but it cannot happen until the alcoholic takes the first step.

Treatment programs and counseling are available to offer extra help for those seeking recovery. Trained professionals can explain the disease and give the alcoholic a safe environment in which to take ownership of the disease and the recovery. Treatment programs give the alcoholic an opportunity to meet others in recovery. Chapter five will offer ideas on what to look for in a treatment program or counseling. But in the end, the alcoholic is the only one who can choose to find recovery.

While it is crucial for the alcoholic to recover, he or she is not the only one enduring a debilitating difficulty. The spouse of the alcoholic suffers, too.

Chapter Three

# Understanding the Spouse of an Alcoholic

# Understanding the Spouse of An Alcoholic

*"I know well the plans I have in mind for you," [says the LORD]; "plans for your welfare and not for woe, so as to give you a future of hope. When you call me, and come and pray to me, I will listen to you."*

JEREMIAH 29:11–12

Alcoholism casts a shadow of uncertainty over the lives of those close to the alcoholic. The questions they often ask themselves are difficult to answer: *How long will this drinking go on? Will he ever get violent when he drinks? What mood is she going to be in when she walks through the door tonight? Why even go to the party? He/She will only get drunk and make fools out of us, as usual!*

While the situations and details might vary from person to person, the themes of those questions are familiar to all spouses of alcoholics. Their lives revolve around the question, "What's the next crisis?"

The alcoholic is not the only one who suffers from the disease of alcoholism. Data shows that each alcoholic affects at least four other people, but typically the spouse's life is the one most significantly damaged by alcoholism. The effects of this disease can be as severe for the spouse as they are for the alcoholic. The name of the spouse's condition is codependency.

## Codependency Defined

Codependency is "ill-health or maladaptive or problematic behavior that is associated with living, working with or otherwise being close to a person with alcoholism," according to Charles L. Whitfield, MD, who specializes in childhood trauma and addictions, including alcoholism. He wrote *Healing the Child Within: Discovery and Recovery for Adult Children of Dysfunctional Families.*

Chapter one described the different facets of the alcoholic's life that are altered by the disease. The physical facet, the presence of alcohol in the body or the actual drinking, constitutes part of the picture. Because the spouse is so close to the alcoholic, he or she cannot help feeling the effects of the drinking and will inevitably alter his or her life according to the ebb and flow of the disease.

## Three Examples of Codependent Behavior

For John and Martha, a married couple, John's drinking is usually the main issue in family arguments. They are planning a party to celebrate the fortieth wedding anniversary of Martha's parents. John and Martha come from large families and have friends who enjoy a good time.

As the date for the party draws near, Martha is increasingly on edge, wondering what will happen if John drinks too much at the party. He promised he won't overdo it, but she has heard that promise before and doubts he'll keep it.

Martha comes up with a plan to make sure he keeps

his promise. She asks her brother to watch John and keep him away from the liquor. She was careful not to let John's drinking companions get invited to the party. She gives the bartender strict instructions not to let John drink too much, and she constantly reminds John about his promise. By the day of the party, she wishes she had never consented to have it in the first place. For Martha, a cloud of doom hovers over the reception hall. The worry and "disaster planning" have caused her to lose sight of the reason for having the party: her parents' anniversary.

John has problems caused by alcohol, yet Martha is planning an event around him and his predicted behavior. This is just one example of how codependency shows itself, and though it is relatively tame, it illustrates how alcohol is the center of Martha's life as much as it is the center of John's. Codependency is revealed on special occasions, like at Martha's party, but it also is present every day.

o o o

Bill rushes home from work every evening afraid of what he might find at home. His wife, Sylvia, started drinking wine to take the edge off the pain from arthritis. What was once a glass or two in the evening has become a bottle or two, beginning in the afternoon.

Their teenagers often come home to find Mom seriously inebriated. Bill gets home, starts dinner, and if the children bring up Mom's problem, he brushes them off, saying, "Mom is fine. Her 'medicine' makes her sleepy. Let's pitch in and help in the kitchen." Bill is trying to cover for Sylvia and reassure their children, but the effect is enabling Sylvia's drinking and telling the children they aren't seeing what they clearly do see.

○ ○ ○

For her daily survival, Ruth has learned cold beer must be in the refrigerator when her husband, Charlie, gets home from work. While he has never been physically abusive, she has suffered through many long evenings listening to him list what he believes are her inadequacies—with a lack of cold beer being at the top of the list. A beer inventory is a normal part of Ruth's daily routine.

Unfortunately, many people spend a great deal of energy trying to avoid life situations much more severe than these examples. Some codependents fear for their lives and the lives of their children. Others don't know how much longer they will have a place to live or if there will be enough money for bills and food.

## Common Myths Unraveled

Codependents are the victims of the same kinds of mistaken attitudes that hamper the alcoholic's thinking.

Here are three common myths about their spouses and other family members.

**Myth 1:** ***The alcoholic is the only one with the problem.***

On the surface, this statement might seem true. After all, the alcoholic is the one who drinks, and the situation is worse when he or she is drunk. In John and Martha's case, Martha might believe that John is the only one with the problem. However, the extent to which worry over John's behavior overshadowed Martha's enjoyment of her parents' anniversary party illustrates that belief is untrue. Any time another person's life is altered or disturbed by the alcoholic's drinking or fear that the alcoholic may drink, the drinker no longer is the only one with a problem. In the literature on codependency, this codependent attitude is referred to as denial.

**Myth 2:** ***The alcoholic's drinking can be controlled.***

No number of threats, nagging, or emptying of bottles can stop the progression of this disease. These tactics may make a short-term difference, but in the long run, the wounds of mistrust, buried anger, and loneliness will deepen.

The futility of trying to control another's drinking is

evident in the second installment of John and Martha's story. At the party, all of Martha's fears were realized. Her brother, who was supposed to watch John, saw no harm in letting him have a drink or two once the party got under way. The bartender became more uncomfortable with John's threats than with Martha's. Once John had insured his supply of alcohol, he could drink as much as he wanted. In the process, he became loud and obnoxious. To enliven the party, he called friends over. When Martha saw what was happening, she tried to confront John without making a scene in front of her loved ones. A major argument ensued, and the uncomfortable guests made their excuses and left.

On the way home, the argument continued. Martha, hurt and angry that John broke his promise, was livid with her brother and the bartender for letting John's drinking get out of hand and at herself for agreeing to hold the party in the first place. She feared it would turn out like this, and it did. Her efforts to control John—impossible tasks—failed.

Besides being doomed to fail, Martha's attempt to control John's drinking made her look like a persecutor to some people. She may have overheard someone say, "Why doesn't she just leave him alone? His drinking isn't hurting anyone!" In truth, John's drinking is hurting *everyone*. And one way to cope with being hurt is to attack.

The myth of control can play out in various ways. Some codependents try to exert control by playing the martyr. The martyr may say, "I can suffer through this now. Everything will work itself out." Meanwhile, the martyr constantly reminds the alcoholic that he or she is the source of great pain, which deepens the guilt the drinker feels.

Some alcoholics may believe and say that if he or she had a more understanding spouse, the drinking would stop. The codependent who accepts that falsehood as true may try to control by becoming a better person. Trying to shape one's behavior to please the alcoholic is the most destructive control tactic for codependents, as it causes their own self-worth to plummet. They end up carrying the entire load alone. So long as there is a desire to "remake" or change another person, control will be a destructive force for both the alcoholic and the codependent. It pushes the alcoholic further away from those who really care, and it results in inevitable frustration for those trying to help.

**Myth 3: *The alcoholic isn't responsible for the drinking and needs someone to take care of him or her.***

This myth is all about a codependent behavior called enabling. In seeking to avoid pain or trouble, most of us follow our instinct to help others. Unfortunately, good intentions and helping hands often make an alcoholic's problems worse. The power of this myth can be broken by first understanding what enabling is and then avoiding it. If the alcoholic has someone to enable him or her by accepting the blame, posting bail, making excuses, or constructing a secret protective shield around the drinking, the alcoholic is not likely to examine alternatives objectively and knowledgeably so that healthier decisions can be reached.

## Get Help Before Deciding to Help Another

The codependent must begin getting help for himself or herself before making any important decisions about the marriage. Healthy decisions require healthy mindsets. That healthy atmosphere cannot be found in the isolation of the sick home. The best place for the codependent to find help is in Al-Anon. This organization supports spouses and families of an alcoholic. It comprises people from the same or similar living situations who have come together to help one another. Al-Anon is based on the Twelve Steps of Alcoholics Anonymous, presented in chapter two.

In Al-Anon, the spouse works the steps the same way an alcoholic does in AA. The steps are applied directly to the spouse's life. The spouse does *not* work the steps for the alcoholic. The spouse has his or her own issues because the disease that the drinker has brought into the home has led to powerlessness for the spouse. Life for the codependent spouse has become unmanageable, and he or she must look to a higher power and fellow recovering codependents for help. Spouses for whom this chapter rings a bell can find Al-Anon meetings by visiting Al-Anon.org.

Veterans of Twelve-Step programs ask newcomers to give the program a fair chance. One meeting can never heal all the pain or offer solutions to all the problems. Just as the disease did not appear overnight, recovery as an addict or a codependent never happens in a snap. Change is possible, but it can come about only in an atmosphere of trust, affirmation, and challenge. Al-Anon provides the atmosphere to help change become a reality in the life of the codependent.

Chapter Four

# Understanding the Child from an Alcoholic Home

# Understanding the Child from an Alcoholic Home

*[Jesus said,] "Let the children come to me; do not prevent them, for the kingdom of God belongs to such as these." Then he embraced them and blessed them, placing his hands on them.*

MARK 10:14, 16

Children of alcoholics (COA) grow up with a "third party" in the household that they cannot see—alcoholism. This invisible party has more power in their home than any other. It dominates the family. The children experience emotional and physical pain and abandonment as a direct result of this disease. As parents struggle to cope with the affliction, they cannot be fully present to the needs of their growing children. One parent, the alcoholic, has alcohol at the center of his or her life. The other parent, the codependent, is preoccupied with coping with the alcoholism. Often, there isn't much left for either parent to give to the children.

Eleven-year-old Nancy would like to be an active member of her local Scout troop. To participate fully, she needs help from her parents to earn merit badges and take part in other scouting activities. Nancy very often has trouble completing projects. Her parents rarely make it to meetings or ceremonies where parents are invited. Her father is an alcoholic. Her mother is usually preoccupied and often takes her bad moods out on Nancy and other members of the family. Nancy's troop leader notices that something is wrong and that Nancy seemingly has two different personalities. She is outgoing, helpful, and talkative at group meetings, but in the presence of her mother, she is quiet and withdrawn.

When the leader asks Nancy if there is anything she would like to discuss, the girl is unwilling to talk. The leader decides to talk with Nancy's mother. Nancy's mom insists everything is fine.

Typical of children of alcoholic families, Nancy was lost in the shuffle. Her mother didn't notice her problems. She only saw problems with her husband's drinking. With the disease in charge of the home, parents are not sure what it means to be a healthy and functional person. Not having developed those qualities themselves, they can hardly pass them on to their children. Children growing up in alcoholic homes deal with fear, anger, low self-esteem, lack of trust, and isolation which are reinforced by the negative feelings and messages they experience repeatedly throughout their lives.

Children learn to cope with their destructive home environment by following these three unwritten but powerful rules:

- Don't think.
- Don't trust.
- Don't feel.

Claudia Black writes about these three rules in her book *It Will Never Happen to Me*. She refers to them as "the means for survival in the alcoholic home." Living with the "don'ts" has a payoff. Children can put the pain at a distance. Unfortunately, positive feelings are shut out along with negative feelings.

Like the alcoholic and the alcoholic's spouse, the child of an alcoholic lives with prevailing myths. The child may have more difficulty understanding and living with these myths because his or her entire world is (and probably always has been) centered on that invisible family member, alcohol. Here are three of the most common myths that shape the lives of children of alcoholics:

***Myth 1: I can fix whatever is wrong in this house if I am good enough or bad enough.***

A child in an alcoholic home may firmly believe and even say, "Their drinking is my fault. If I were better, the drinking wouldn't be so bad." Because the parents are so involved in dealing with the disease, the gift of nurturing needed to develop a healthy sense of self is absent. As a result, the child comes to believe that he or she is not as good as other people.

The child in the alcoholic home may be shown love at times, but the message often is inconsistent at best. For example, it is difficult for Carrie to believe her father loves her when his drinking appears to be more important to him than she is. Carrie has the added pressure of knowing her mother expects her to do well in school so her father will be proud of her. That message leads Carrie to believe that pride is the same as love or that the only way her father will notice her is when she can do something for him. She learns that love does not come to her simply because she is who she is. It can only come to her through what she does.

This myth can be lived through negative behavior, too. The child might believe a statement like: "My parent's drinking is my fault. I'm always getting into trouble. No matter what I do, I'll never be any good. What's the use in trying?" Whenever Ricky does something he knows he shouldn't have done, he braces himself to hear about all the bad things he has ever done. He knows his alcoholic father uses Ricky's actions as an excuse to drink and will eventually storm out of the house to "calm down" at the corner bar. Ricky knows his mother will follow his father because she thinks he won't get as drunk if she is with him. Ricky is left at home to do whatever he wants. Even though he enjoys the short periods of peace and quiet with his parents out of the house, deep down he believes he is the direct cause of all the unhappiness in the family. During their formative years, these children develop a clouded sense of self. The most significant people in their lives are unable to help them develop as secure human beings.

***Myth 2: No other household is as bad as this one.***

Children who live in alcoholic homes live in fear that their secret will be found out. Because the home environment is so unstable, they learn to guess what is normal or functional. They have skewed reference points, like television shows, for what normal family dynamics look like. Thirty-minute TV episodes often have happy endings. Everyone gets along and is willing to talk. The reality for the child in the home of an alcoholic, however, contradicts that notion. The child learns to work hard to see that the family secrets stay under wraps. Secrets might include physical violence, verbal attacks, and sexual abuse. The sexual abuse may be overt (physical contact) or covert (comments or inappropriate humor).

The destructive result of this myth can be seen in the lives of three children living in the same home, a boy and two girls ages eleven, thirteen, and fourteen. All three were sexually molested by their alcoholic father between the ages of eight and ten. Each child kept the abuse a secret from the other two and from their mother. Each child feared being blamed for the father's actions. Each was unsure of the love of other family members and of the consequences if the secret got out. Eventually, the attempt to keep all the secrets in the alcoholic home leads to loneliness and isolation.

***Myth 3: No one out there can really be trusted.***

The child believes it's best not to talk about the problems at home. People may not understand and may even think there is something wrong with the child because he or she does not come from a perfect home. Attempts to trust others end in disappointment or even more problems. After being hurt often enough, the child learns it's safer not to trust anyone and to rely only on themselves.

Sandy, seventeen, is the oldest of five children. Her mother is an alcoholic. Her father works long hours and is rarely home. The alcoholism had taken charge of the household by the time Sandy was twelve years old. Sandy began to assume many of the tasks her mother neglected. She cooked, cleaned, washed clothes, and cared for her brothers and sisters, doing well at all these things.

Sandy's mother constantly thanked Sandy for all she was doing and promised to make things better. Her father kept telling her how proud he was and reassured her that her mother would pull out of her slump soon. Sandy gave up several opportunities to get involved in after-school activities and to spend time with her friends. She told herself she was needed at home. Besides, it looked as if nothing was going to change. Her mother would never stop drinking, and her father would never do anything to help.

Just before Sandy's sixteenth birthday, however, her mother entered the hospital for treatment of alcoholism. Sandy saw a ray of hope. She noticed a change in both her mother and father when her mother came home from the hospital. Her mother began to take an interest in the household. Her father was spending more time at home. The counselor explained to them that it would take time, but things would get better. Sandy, however, would not let herself believe this promise. Her experiences had taught her not to trust anyone but herself. Although Sandy's mother has been in recovery for over a year, Sandy is still waiting for everything to crumble and return to the way it was before.

## The Four Roles of the COA

Children from alcoholic homes come by their feelings and beliefs honestly. But they have merely found a way to cope with life that works for them. Unfortunately, they end up surviving in life rather than fully living it. Survival is an important attribute in the alcoholic family. The children in these homes typically develop one of four roles in the family system to get through the pain and survive: the Hero, the Scapegoat, the Lost Child, or the Mascot.

## The Hero

In this identity, often adopted by the oldest child, the child is responsible, well-liked, outgoing, and looks as if she or he has everything under control. Despite the bright, positive exterior, however, the Hero doesn't really believe she or he has self-worth. Hero kids are aware of their imperfections and fear them.

## The Scapegoat

Often associated with the second child or one of the middle children, the Scapegoat is usually in trouble at home, with friends, and in school. This child has been told he or she is bad so often that it is difficult for him or her to believe otherwise. Actions and decisions constantly reinforce this idea. The negative externals reinforce what Scapegoat kids feel inside.

## The Lost Child

Typically the quiet one who spends as much time alone as possible, the Lost Child has found that the best way to stay safe is to become invisible, and she or he finds comfort in fantasies of a conflict-free home where everyone loves one another. Lost Children often escape into books, television, and their own daydreams. Inside, these kids are usually lonely and afraid.

## The Mascot

This role resembles what we know as the family clown. A Mascot can get a laugh or smile from just about anyone. He or she likes to keep the mood light and free of tension. The Mascot has trouble sitting still, but on the inside, this child is often deeply hurt and running from the pain.

## Examples of the Four Roles

Four children come home from school one day to find their mother home early from work and sitting at the kitchen table with a large bottle of wine. She tells them she's been fired from her job but doesn't say why. The children suspect it was because of her drinking.

Hannah immediately begins to give orders to the others and starts checking the kitchen to see what the family will have for supper. She tells her brother, Sam, to do the breakfast dishes and tidy the living room. Sam replies he has better things to do and picks up his phone to call some of his friends. His mother begins ranting that he had better stay away from those kids who always get him in trouble. Larry, the third child, has turned on the television and won't even consider doing what Sam won't do. Hannah knows she can count on Mary, the youngest, to give her a hand.

While they are cleaning the kitchen and preparing supper, Mary tells her mother and Hannah about all the things that happened to her at school that day. All four children are afraid of what their father's reaction is going to be when he gets home. This might even be the final blowout they have all been afraid was coming.

Hannah the Hero deals with her fears by taking charge. Sam the Scapegoat sees this as an opportunity to be with friends his parents don't approve of and maybe have a little fun in the bargain. Larry the Lost Child escapes into his favorite television program, where he knows everything will turn out all right in the end. Mary the Mascot feels the tension and thinks, *If I can keep everyone entertained, I can release the tension and it won't be so bad when Dad gets home.*

It's important to understand that these roles are not play-acting. They are a means of survival. By seeing which behavior works and which does not, each child learns what to do to get through the next crisis. Once a role is learned, it forms a protective shell around the child, who then carries it into all areas of his or her life. Those feelings can be conquered through breaking down the shell, but that can only happen in an affirming and supportive environment.

## COAs, Alateens, and ACOAs

Children growing up in alcoholic homes deal with fear, anger, low self-esteem, lack of trust, and isolation which are reinforced by the negative feelings and messages in which to explore and deal with the past. Attendees at Twelve-Step meetings for children of alcoholics (COAs) and teenage children of alcoholics (Alateens) hear from others what it is like to live in the present and look to the future with hope.

Using the Twelve Steps, children, teens, and adult children of alcoholics (ACOA) can learn to think, trust, and feel in positive ways. As with AA and Al-Anon, COAs and ACOAs are asked to give the program a full effort. One meeting cannot help people work through all of life's issues that have been influenced by living day after day in the home of an alcoholic. It took a long time for the disease to do its work on the alcoholic and the spouse. Recovery for the children takes time, too.

## Thirteen Characteristics of Adults Who Grew Up in an Alcoholic Home

1. Inability to discern what normal behavior is.
2. Difficulty following a project through from beginning to end.
3. Proclivity to lie when it would be just as easy to tell the truth.
4. Ability to judge themselves without mercy.
5. Find it difficult to indulge in a good time and have fun.
6. Tendency to take themselves very seriously.
7. Struggle to initiate and maintain intimate relationships.
8. Don't respond well to change, may even overreact to changes they don't have control over.
9. A constant need to seek approval and affirmation.
10. Likely feel they are different from other people.
11. Lean toward extremes in terms of responsibility or lack thereof.

12. Are extremely loyal, even in the face of evidence that the loyalty is undeserved.

13. Impulsive, even locking themselves into a course of action without giving serious consideration to alternative behaviors or possible consequences.

All these characteristics are grounded in the negative feelings buried under the protective shell that their assumed roles provide. They also all relate, one way or another, to the three unspoken rules in the previous section: "Don't think. Don't trust. Don't feel." Outwardly, adult children from alcoholic homes (ACOAs) appear functional. Their coping skills are refined because they have learned what works and what does not.

*Source:* Adult Children of Alcoholics, © *1983, 1990 Janet Geringer Woititz, Health Communications Inc.*

Chapter Five

# Climbing Off the Roller Coaster

# Climbing Off the Roller Coaster

*May the God of hope fill you with all joy and peace in believing, so that you may abound in hope by the power of the holy Spirit.*

ROMANS 15:13

Those who live with alcoholism do not have to live in despair. The roller coaster can be stopped. Life can be better than it ever was. This may sound like a happy ending to a fairy tale, but it is not. There are simple solutions. However, it's important to understand they are simple, not easy.

Recovery is a personal choice. Each person must decide for himself or herself to overcome the addiction. With that decision, a bridge is built to lead to a renewed life and recovery. What about a starting point? Three valuable options in this personal choice are the Twelve-Step program, professional counseling, and crisis intervention.

## The Twelve-Step Program

The program is more a necessity than an option. The previous chapters cite brief descriptions of different Twelve-Step groups: AA, Al-Anon, COA, Alateen, and ACOA. These groups offer necessary help for those suffering from alcoholism—alcoholics and their family and friends.

Newcomers walking into their first meetings are looking for change. They know life cannot go on as it has. Change can be frightening. Because a safety net of anonymity surrounds each of the groups, newcomers are reaching into the unknown for change. Once there, however, they find possibilities for life renewal that they may never have believed possible—one day at a time.

Alcoholics and their family and friends find others at Twelve-Step meetings who are at different stages in living with this disease. Groups are places to listen to the stories of others and learn what they do to fight the daily battles against alcoholism. The group is a safe place to ask for help and to share individual stories and struggles.

## Professional Counseling

Individual or family counseling can be a tremendous resource to begin and strengthen recovery. I suggest it here as a supplement to, not a replacement for, the Twelve-Step program. Counselors offer a trained and objective ear to alcoholics and their families working on specific issues. Many hospitals offer in-patient treatment programs for alcoholics and their family members.

Vital criteria for selecting a treatment program of high quality are its reliance on the Twelve-Step program as the road to recovery from alcoholism and family programs designed to help everyone affected by the disease.

When choosing an individual counselor, remember that not every counselor, psychologist, or psychiatrist is qualified to work with people who suffer from alcoholism and codependency. Ask if the therapist is familiar with Twelve-Step programs. If not, it might be better to find someone who is.

One drawback to professional counseling can be cost. Families afflicted by alcoholism often do not have stable finances, and treatment can be expensive. But just as the expense of such life-sustaining items as food, utilities, and housing is necessary, the expense involved in treatment is worth it. Most health insurance plans cover some or all of the costs involved in alcoholism treatment. The coverage varies according to policies. For those with no insurance, there are programs that are free or on a sliding scale according to an individual's ability to pay.

## Crisis Intervention

Earlier I noted how alcoholism progresses from bad to worse for everyone involved. However, people do not have to sit idly and watch their lives disintegrate. One formal, positive way of altering or even stopping the progression of the disease is called crisis intervention, a process designed to gather family and friends with the intent of formally confronting the alcoholic about the effects of his or her drinking. A sample of an actual intervention, from Fr. Denis Ryan, is at the front of this book.

An intervention's hoped-for outcome is to "raise the bottom" of alcoholism's progression. If the progression of the disease follows its own course, "hitting bottom" can come only after there is serious damage to the alcoholic's family, friends, career, and his or her own health.

Every participant in the intervention plays one of three roles: the facilitator, the family members and other significant people in the alcoholic's life, and the active alcoholic. The facilitator is trained in the process of interventions and directs the process of preparation and the actual intervention. Do not attempt an intervention without someone who has been properly trained. Family members or other well-meaning friends attempting this activity on their own could do more harm than good. Facilitators should not lead an intervention if they are close enough to the alcoholic to be a participant.

The facilitator will prepare the participants for the intervention and also choose the time and place. A time will be selected when the alcoholic will be sober and able to understand what he or she is being told. The place might be the facilitator's office or, depending on the circumstances, it may take place in the home of the alcoholic. The alcoholic will be told whatever is necessary to get him or her into the place where the intervention will be held. A trained facilitator is qualified to identify when and where the intervention is to take place.

At the intervention, the participants take turns presenting the alcoholic with a prepared statement of specific times or events when their lives were altered because of the drinking. The classic "I statement" is often used, which focuses on the presenter's feelings, rather than making accusations. "I was sad when you missed my recital." "I was scared and angry when I found you passed out in the car." And so on. The participants end their statement by telling the alcoholic how much they care, and then asking the alcoholic to get help.

These statements are not spontaneous ramblings. They are carefully worded so as not to be accusations made to inflict guilt. Alcoholism is not mentioned because the purpose of intervention is not diagnosis.

When the intervention is over, family members and friends should know they have done everything possible to help in a healthy manner. They have asked that the alcoholic get help and given him or her a way to get that help. Whether or not the person gets help, the drinking is no longer a forbidden subject or a secret. If they haven't already done so, those most affected can get help for themselves. Interventions are complicated, but the benefits are positive and powerful for everyone involved.

## Intervention Scenario

Henry is a married man in his middle forties, the father of two children. He has a son who is married and lives in another part of the city. His daughter still lives at home and will be married soon. The family has noticed that Henry's drinking is getting worse. He was arrested three times in the last year for driving while intoxicated. He continues to miss work, although he has used up all his sick days, thus putting his job in jeopardy. When he is not at work, he rarely goes anywhere and complains that the people he used to call friends act self-righteous about his drinking.

His wife, Doris, has been attending Al-Anon meetings and getting personal counseling to deal with all the pressures in her life. In spite of the help, she is getting for herself, everything is getting worse. She knows some action needs to be taken. Her counselor suggests an intervention for Henry, and she agrees that it would be a good idea. The counselor gives Doris a general explanation of the process and asks her which people in Henry's life would be appropriate to participate. Doris mentions her children, Henry's boss, and his brother, Carl. They decide to arrange a meeting with all the possible participants to discuss the intervention.

As Doris calls people to set up the meeting, she finds

she is getting a mixed reaction from those she thought would be enthusiastic about participating. Her son tells her he got out of the house so he would no longer have to deal with the problems caused by his father's drinking and wants to be left out of it. Her daughter, Susan, on the other hand, is eager to help. Henry's brother, Carl, hesitates because he is angry at Henry. But he consents to give it a try. Henry's boss, Frank, thinks it is a great idea. He tells Doris about Henry's troubles at work and explains that Henry will lose his job if he doesn't change. During their conversation, Doris learns that, as a recovering alcoholic himself, Frank is quite understanding.

At the first meeting, the counselor explains the intervention process. Susan is afraid everything might backfire and ruin her wedding. Carl wants to yell at Henry for the three times he had to bail him out of jail. Doris is confused and feels desperate. Frank is enthusiastic and confident in the process.

Each person is asked to do three things.

1. Make a list of specific times when Henry's drinking caused problems directly involving the person making the statement.
2. List reasons for being part of the intervention. These will form the basis of the caring statement.

3. Attend Al-Anon to start to learn more about the disease and develop a support system. In short, ask for help.

The next meeting is a time for formal practice. The room is set up as it will be for the real intervention. The group decides the order in which the statements will be given. As each person reads his or her statement, the counselor helps with the wording. Susan focuses on her love for her father rather than on fear about her wedding. Carl lists the three times he bailed Henry out of jail and tells how concerned he is that his brother had to spend time in jail. Frank brings attendance records from work and affirms Henry's attitude when sober. Doris lists examples of the distance in their relationship that Henry's drinking caused.

In this meeting, the counselor discusses "what if" statements. These are honest consequences about what will happen if Henry does not choose to get help. They are not empty threats. They are the reality of what will happen if he does not get help. The counselor explains that each person must be sure he or she will follow through with whatever statement is made. The participants leave the meeting promising to think carefully about the repercussions behind their statements and to attend Al-Anon meetings in the interim. They decide to meet a half-hour before the formal intervention to discuss their statements and ask questions.

On the day of the intervention, Henry is shocked to find everyone in the same room. He appears frightened when he finds out the reason for the meeting. He follows the instructions of the counselor and listens quietly to what his friends and family have to say. He realizes when they are all finished that the decision is up to him. Each person has told Henry what he or she will do if he does not get help. Susan will not let him come to her wedding. Carl will no longer bail him out of jail. His boss will fire him. Doris will no longer watch him drink. She has decided that if he continues to drink, she wants a legal separation. She did not feel she could say she would divorce him, but she knows she cannot stay in the same house and watch him drink.

In the end, all the participants could say that they did everything possible to help Henry. They each told him they cared. They set up boundaries so he knew what was acceptable to them and what they would no longer tolerate moving forward. Of course, no two interventions are ever the same. The number of preparation meetings may vary according to the needs of the participants. Henry's response is not included in the example because the point of this section of the book is to discuss how to intervene. The choice is up to the subject of the intervention. Accountability is important in recovery. In this example, Henry's family, brother, and employer had done all they could. The intervention was successful in that the family members got help for themselves and brought the secret into the open. Even if Henry continues to drink, it will never be the same again.

### *Confrontation Guidance from our Lord*

Jesus describes something very much like an intervention when he teaches the disciples how to confront someone about their behavior.

> *[Jesus said,] "If your brother sins [against you], go and tell him his fault between you and him alone. If he listens to you, you have won over your brother. If he does not listen, take one or two others along with you, so that 'every fact may be established on the testimony of two or three witnesses.' If he refuses to listen to them, tell the church. If he refuses to listen even to the church, then treat him as you would a Gentile or a tax collector."*
>
> *Matthew 18:15–17*

## How to Find Someone to Help

If you feel there is a problem with drinking in your life (either your own or that of someone you care about), you can begin to look for help in several places. You may know someone who is already involved in one of the Twelve-Step programs: AA, Al-Anon, COA, Alateen, or ACOA. You can find contact information for those groups online. While people in these groups will not be able to serve as a counselor or therapist (those are not their roles), they can offer direction for help. They may even share their own stories.

Pastors or ministers will also likely have a list they use to refer parishioners who are finding that drinking is a problem in their lives. The basic rule in asking for help applies to the clergy, too. A pastor's familiarity with Twelve-Step programs indicates his or her knowledge in this area.

Many employers have an Employee Assistance Program (EAP) as part of the benefit package for their companies. An EAP is set up to help employees with many different issues. Because alcoholism has a definite impact on the workplace, the EAP should have resources to offer. Each person must decide for herself or himself when it is time to get help. There are qualified people willing to help those who ask for it. Those living in the hell of this disease find that asking for help is the first and often the most difficult obstacle to overcome.

# Conclusion

Alcoholism, a form of chemical dependence, is a destructive disease for which there is no quick cure. The lives of many are torn apart as a direct result of one person's use of mood-altering chemicals. The outlook does not have to be completely hopeless. But a happy ending—or more accurately, a new beginning—is possible.

For the alcoholics reading this, your disease did not develop overnight, and the same is true for arresting it and reversing its effects. As difficult as it can be, recovery begins with facing the hard facts, examining the damage to your life, and admitting the pain caused to others, often to your family and closest friends.

Recovery is not magic or immediate. You must believe and live with integrity, admit your personal limitations, rely on a Power outside of yourself, and honestly confess to others your struggles. This life is possible through a Twelve-Step program where you are challenged to embrace one step at a time, one day at a time. God bless you.

# Resources

# What Is AA?

Alcoholics Anonymous is an international fellowship of men and women who have had a drinking problem. It is nonprofessional, self-supporting, multiracial, apolitical, and available almost everywhere. There are no age or education requirements. Membership is open to anyone who wants to do something about his or her drinking problem.

Since the book *Alcoholics Anonymous* first appeared in 1939, this basic text has helped millions of men and women recover from alcoholism. Currently available in the General Service Conference-approved fourth edition, the *Big Book* contains the stories of the co-founders, as well as many members of diverse backgrounds who have found recovery in the worldwide fellowship.

o o o

**THE TWELVE STEPS OF ALCOHOLICS ANONYMOUS (text on pages 39–40)** are principles, spiritual in nature, which, if practiced as a way of life, can expel the obsession to drink and enable the sufferer to become happily and usefully whole.

## Twelve Traditions of AA (Short Form)

AA's twelve traditions apply to the life of the fellowship itself. They outline the means by which AA maintains its unity and relates itself to the world and the way it lives and grows.

1. Our common welfare should come first; personal recovery depends upon AA unity.
2. For our group purpose there is but one ultimate authority—a loving God as He may express Himself in our group conscience. Our leaders are but trusted servants; they do not govern.
3. The only requirement for AA membership is a desire to stop drinking.
4. Each group should be autonomous except in matters affecting other groups or AA as a whole.
5. Each group has but one primary purpose—to carry its message to the alcoholic who still suffers.
6. An AA group ought never endorse, finance, or lend the AA name to any related facility or outside enterprise, lest problems of money, property, and prestige divert us from our primary purpose.

7. Every AA group ought to be fully self-supporting, declining outside contributions.
8. Alcoholics Anonymous should remain forever nonprofessional, but our service centers may employ special workers.
9. AA, as such, ought never be organized; but we may create service boards or committees directly responsible to those they serve.
10. Alcoholics Anonymous has no opinion on outside issues; hence the AA name ought never be drawn into public controversy.
11. Our public relations policy is based on attraction rather than promotion; we need always maintain personal anonymity at the level of press, radio, and films.
12. Anonymity is the spiritual foundation of all our Traditions, ever reminding us to place principles before personalities.



*Source:* Verbatim from *AA.org*

## Guides

Excerpts from Liguori Publications products on spiritual healing follow. To order, please visit Liguori.org.

# An Ever-Present Help

Likewise the Spirit helps us in our weakness; for we do not know how to pray as we ought, but that very Spirit intercedes with sighs too deep for words. And God, who searches the heart, knows what is the mind of the Spirit, because the Spirit intercedes for the saints according to the will of God (see Romans 8).

What then are we to say about these things? If God is for us, who is against us? He who did not withhold his own Son, but gave him up for all of us, will he not with him also give us everything else? Who will bring any charge against God's elect? It is God who justifies. Who is to condemn? It is Christ Jesus, who died, yes, who was raised, who is at the right hand of God, who indeed intercedes for us.

No, in all these things we are more than conquerors through him who loved us. For I am convinced that neither death, nor life, nor angels, nor rulers, nor things present, nor things to come, nor powers, nor height, nor depth, nor anything else in all creation, will be able to separate us from the love of God in Christ Jesus our Lord.

○ ○ ○

People with diabetes don't hang their heads when their sugar levels rise or fall. They look at their diets, or stress, or exercise, and they make adjustments. They consult with health experts and may decide to attend an educational support group. They know recovery means continually learning how to live daily with their disease. We, too, need to learn to live with the disease. And once we acknowledge that our addiction keeps us from being who we want to be, we are in recovery.

*You who dwell in the shelter of the Most High,*
*who abide in the shade of the Almighty,*
*Say to the* Lord, *"My refuge and fortress,*
*my God in whom I trust."*
*He will rescue you from the fowler's snare,*
*from the destroying plague,*
*He will shelter you with his pinions,*
*and under his wings you may take refuge;*
*his faithfulness is a protecting shield.*

*Psalm 91:1–4*

## About Prayer

When I pray to "be released from the fowler's snare"
    I pray that God's promise is clear to me in what
    I will meet that day,
that I will be able to manage it with his grace,
and that I will feel his presence when I need his
    strength.
It works in us throughout the day without our even
    being conscious of it.

Source: *Broken By Addition, Blessed By God: A Woman's Path to Sustained Recovery*, © 2010 Penny Mary Hauser, MSN, Liguori Publications

## Getting Well, Staying Well

In John 5:6, Jesus asks the paralyzed man at the pool at Bethesda, "Do you want to get well?" That question is extremely important in the healing of addictions, because if you do not really desire wholeness, any attempt at recovery will be futile. Why would anyone not want to get well? One man said that the cure was worse than the disease. Another reason could be that we complain, but we quickly become comfortable with our "demons"; they provide us with some kind of seen or unseen protection from whatever is assaulting our spirits and overwhelming us. Perhaps the pain of the attack is too intense; we need those demons and will not be able to part with them until we are thoroughly committed to recovery, by replacing the addictive substances or behaviors with an intimate, vibrant, and deepened relationship with God. Change is hard, uncomfortable, demanding, and it shows us things about ourselves that maybe we'd rather not see. But, those hesitations must be coupled with our innate flexibility and ability to change: It is never too late. We always have a choice.

## Prayer

Lord God, you made us weak so we might know your
strength.
You made us indecisive so we might know your
faithfulness.
Jesus says, "I am the way, the truth, and the life."
Give us strength for the journey and
steadfast confidence in your presence beside us. Amen.

Source: *Praying Throughout the Day: A Book of Hours for Those with Addictions*, © 2007 Harriet Roberts, Liguori Publications (814792)

o o o

Addictions of all types thrive in a culture marked by high levels of feelings of alienation, stress, and loneliness. Being caught in addiction causes despair, self-loathing, and shame. This pamphlet examines the reasons for addiction, why it breeds self-contempt, and that through God's love we can know peace, serenity, and our true self-worth.

Source: *Finding a Spiritual Path Through an Addictive Culture* by Raymond D. Dlugos, OSA, PhD, © 2009 Liguori Publications (pamphlet 817830)

o o o

Illnesses often take a spiritual toll that we are not used to confronting. As we seek comfort and healing, we struggle to find meaningful words to pray. This pamphlet offers thirty prayers, each framed by a quote from the Psalms, for facing the spiritual trials of illness or a hospital stay.

Source: *Prayers for Healing Body and Soul* by Sally Macke, © 2011 Liguori Publications (pamphlet 820052)

# A Healing Ritual For Addicts (and those who love them)

This ritual from *Everyday Catholic* may be used for praying alone or with others. The wording of prayers is taken from the source.

## Preparation

Place a large bowl of water, a rock for each participant, a lighted candle and a Bible on a prayer table.

## Opening Song

Sing "Create in Me" by Bob Hurd
(or other suitable music).

## The Serenity Prayer

God, grant me the serenity
To accept the things I cannot change;
Courage to change the things I can;
And wisdom to know the difference.

Living one day at a time;
Enjoying one moment at a time;
Accepting hardships as the pathway to peace;
Taking, as he did, this sinful world
As it is, not as I would have it;

Trusting that he will make all things right
If I surrender to his will;
So that I may be reasonably happy in this life
And supremely happy with him
Forever and ever in the next. Amen.

## Scripture

> *Trust in the LORD with all your heart,*
> *on your own intelligence do not rely;*
> *In all your ways be mindful of him,*
> *and he will make straight your paths.*

*Proverbs 3:5–6*

## Ritual

Pick up a rock. The rock is a symbol of a hard place in your life, an overwhelming wound, addiction, loss of freedom or dysfunction. It might be overeating, spending too much, alcohol, gambling, loss of control or bad temper. Let us sit in quiet for a moment and each name the rock for ourselves.

*(Sit in silence for a few moments.)*

You are invited to come forward and place your rock in the bowl of water. It was through the waters of Baptism that God claimed you as his own. As you release your rock into the water, ask God to heal that place in your heart that suffers from the pain of addiction. Then, sign yourself with this water as a reminder of your Baptism, that you are God's own. Pray to God for healing.

## Closing Prayer

O Divine Redeemer, take our fragile spirits and restore them. Give wholeness to the broken. Remove any anger, resentment or fear that keeps us from freedom. Gently enfold us in your love, so that we may know your healing. Amen.

Source: *Everyday Catholic* by Jeanne Hunt, April 2009 (Liguori Publications)

○ ○ ○

**Fr. Ted Lawson, CSsR**, is the director of the Redemptorist Retreat Center in Oconomowoc, Wisconsin. While in graduate school, Fr. Ted received addiction-counseling education at the Clinical Training Program for Addiction Counselors. He never ceases to be amazed by the inspiring stories of the people he encounters when he is called to direct retreats, offer days of recollection, and preach parish missions and novenas nationwide. Fr. Ted is particularly devoted to making known Our Mother of Perpetual Help, the "Window to the Gospel."

Printed in the USA
CPSIA information can be obtained
at www.ICGtesting.com
CBHW021213281024
16415CB00003B/11

9 780764 828645